How to furnish your home for practically nothing.

Anita Bilkey

Dedication

To my incredible husband Paul, who always supports me in my adventures, I am so thankful for your love and support.

To my children, who have given me such encouragement throughout my journey, you have brought such incredible joy to our family and I am in awe of the amazing individuals you are becoming with each passing year.

Acknowledgement

This book would never have seen the light of day without the great many people.

Thank you to my book designer, Scott Bilkey, and my copy editors, Adam Bilkey and Erin McWhinney, and others without whom this book would not be as beautiful or read as well.

Thank you to Tess Bilkey, for her support and encouragement.

Thank you to my husband, Paul for his support.

ISBN 978-0-6450808-0-3

Some images have been taken from public domain libraries such as Pixabay, Pexels etc.

All text and remaining photographs copyright © 2021 by Anita Bilkey

All rights reserved

This book or parts may not be reproduced in any form without permission of the author.

Published by A B Interiors

Printed in Australia

First Edition

Book design by Scott Bilkey

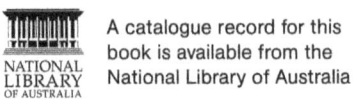

A catalogue record for this book is available from the National Library of Australia

What's in this book?

Introduction	**5**
Chapter 1 - Basic facts	**6**
Chapter 2 - The experiment	**10**
Chapter 3 - Style	**14**
Scandinavian style	18
Hamptons style	21
Retro style	22
Industrial style	25
Boho style	26
Coastal style	29
Chapter 4 - Getting started	**30**
Chapter 5 - Finding your pieces	**34**
Furniture	36
Handles	37
Beds	38
Sofas and couches	39
Linen and blinds	41
Accessories and artwork	43
Rugs	46
Lamps	48
Kitchenware	49
Large electrical items	50
Pickup or delivery	51
Using your imagination	53
Realising you bought the wrong item	54
Chapter 6 - Painting	**56**
Paint, paint and more paint!	58
Some rules on preparing furniture for painting	60
Brushes and rollers	61
Primer	62
Gloss levels and colour for water-based enamels	63
The painting process	66
Whitewashing	70
Distressing your piece	71
Putting it into practice	72
Chapter 7 - Upholstery	**74**
Getting started in upholstery	76
Fabric	78
Chapter 8 - Budget	**80**
Bargin buys	84
Chapter 9 - Before and afters	**88**

Introduction

Throughout my career as an interior designer, I have always been fascinated by furniture. This came from an artistic interest that surfaced when I was a child.

I didn't start out as an interior designer – I realised later in my career that I wanted to do something I was passionate about and interior design filled that void. So, I went back to college and received my qualifications, and there I learnt all I could about the industry. When I started researching furniture designers, I found I loved how they used form, colour and texture to create their pieces, which inspired my love of furniture.

After years of experience in the industry, I have found that I can inspire my clients and find ways to help them achieve the look they are after, within their budget. I encourage my clients to look at what they already have to see if they can adapt any furniture or décor items into the style they want to achieve. This also means looking at items they have hidden away in the cupboard. Sometimes, all that is needed is one accent piece to adapt the other items into their new style.

Some of my clients have been interested in learning how to paint their own furniture to update their look, and have even asked if I would paint the furniture for them. Alas, I am not a professional painter and I have found myself explaining how to paint the item and what the client needs to do to complete the project.

I realised there was a need for this kind of information. The average person could learn how to repurpose their furniture themselves, and in doing so would help the planet by recycling. The thought of a perfectly good piece going to the dump makes me cringe!

Then I started to think, 'What if …?' What if furniture could be repurposed on a larger scale? Was it possible to furnish a whole house for practically nothing?

Chapter 1

Basic facts

Basic facts

FACT

Around **85%** of all furniture we put on the kerb ends up in landfill and is not recycled. Much of this is non-solid wood furniture that is flooding the market.

From War on Waste, Australian Broadcasting Corporation

FACT

According to an Australian Government review of the effects of furniture manufacturing on the environment, the use of timber is less damaging than the use of other materials such as metal and plastic.

From the Review of the Environmental Impact of Wood Compared with Alternative Products Used in the Production of Furniture by the Forest and Wood Products Research and Development Corporation and the Australian Government

FACT

We are increasingly persuaded by TV renovation shows and social media to update old furniture and remodel our homes, and this is adding more furniture to landfill than ever before.

In the US, the EPA reported that furniture accounted for 9.8 million tons (4.1 per cent) of household waste, and that was in 2009!

From PlanetSave.com, 'EPA reports 9.8 million tons per year in furniture waste'

Basic facts

FACT
Solid wood that is sustainably sourced is better for the environment than engineered wood, as it uses less energy and none of the toxic chemicals that are used in the manufacture of engineered wood.

*From QuercusLiving.co.uk,
'Why solid wood is better than engineered wood'*

FACT
Solid wood is better value for money, as it lasts longer and can be resanded and refinished multiple times. Engineered wood is inferior and doesn't age as well as solid wood

*From QuercusLiving.co.uk,
'Why solid wood is better than engineered wood'*

Chapter 2

The experiment

The experiment

Refurnishing your home to keep up with the ever-changing style landscape can be an expensive pastime. But you know what? It doesn't have to be!

Anyone can create an interior with lots of money, but what if you only have a small budget? I have worked in commercial, residential and retail industries with kitchen manufacturers, home builders and tile and furniture suppliers, and I understand that quality does come at a price. But I also believe that we can recycle other people's trash and create our own treasure.

Creating a magazine-worthy look when buying second-hand is surprisingly easy, and I will show you just how easy it is.

I began by wondering if it was even possible to furnish a three-bedroom home by upcycling furniture or buying second-hand, and I wondered what it would cost. So I decided to take some of my own pieces of furniture and adapt them to meet my needs and style.

I experimented by painting a small piece to start with, and chose a wooden coffee table. I enjoyed it so much, I wanted to do more! It blew my mind how simple and easy it was to repurpose and update pieces, and it also opened my eyes to the appalling amount of furniture that ends up in landfill.

My experiment developed a dual purpose: I would be getting the most out of a small budget and helping the planet along the way. I did the sums and found I could furnish a three-bedroom home for a mind-blowing $2,000! What a bargain!

I found the whole process challenging, creative and fun, and I'm sure you will too. So keep reading and start your journey to furnishing your home for practically nothing!

The experiment

Chapter 3

Style

Style

Before we talk about furniture, it is really important to find your style. I can't stress this enough!

When I ask clients what style and feel they are trying to achieve, they can struggle with this question. Knowing your style will give you a roadmap for which pieces you need, the colours you should choose and the form and style of your furniture. And the only way to find your style is to do your research!

There are so many styles to choose from. Here we will look at some of the most popular: Scandinavian, Hamptons, Retro, Industrial, Boho, and Coastal.
Each one of these looks takes inspiration from older styles and transitions with each phase. Transitional interiors combine traditional and modern elements, which offers plenty of flexibility when you are trying to create a cohesive design that suits your style.

If you don't feel that your style is reflected here, hop online and research the look that most appeals to you by searching for images of, say, living room interiors. Once you find a style, check out the elements that make up that style by looking closely at the furniture, the colours, and the shape, form and texture of the items.

Styles are made up of multiple elements. Each piece only needs to have one or two of the style elements, and the combination of several of these pieces will make up a style. For example, you could have a white coffee table and a wooden lamp to reflect a Scandinavian style.

Keep in mind that you can transition across two styles if they are similar or you want that eclectic look. For example, a square wooden coffee table with square legs doesn't really fit a Scandinavian style and is more of a Hamptons style. However, you could make it work if you wanted to add a more industrial feel to your Scandinavian style. Leave the timber top unpainted and paint the legs of the table black. Or, if the shade of the timber is not to your liking, you could paint it, lime-wax it or whitewash it.

The same goes for a round coffee table with round legs. If you want a Hamptons style, painting it white will give it more of that classic art deco feel.

Style

When working with existing pieces, it is important to understand that you need to be flexible. Sometimes, the pieces you've got just won't do. If you feel you need a round coffee table rather than the square one you have, you can sell it and buy one that you prefer second-hand.

Style is so important for guiding your choices. So, let's talk about your style!

Scandinavian style

Scandinavian design is minimalist, with clean lines, neutral colours and a simple palette. It has a strong focus on simplicity and function; interiors are bright, airy, and practical.

Elements of Scandinavian style:
- Open spaces uncluttered by furniture or accessories
- Light, muted colours and plenty of natural light
- Practical furniture that serves a purpose
- A celebration of nature, with a strong focus on pale timbers and greenery
- Natural timbers and fabrics
- Pastel colours for interest
- Matt crisp whites
- Copper accents
- Textured rugs
- Timber floors with no wall-to-wall carpets
- Round or oval tables with round legs

Hamptons style

This a classic look, with country style overtones reflected in cabinets. The interiors have a simple palette and classical and refined décor with personal touches.

Elements of Hamptons style:
- Open spaces
- Light, muted colours and plenty of natural light
- Classic furniture in natural tones or white
- Bleached and white timbers
- Blue accent colours for interest
- Matt crisp whites
- Black or silver accents
- Oak floors with carpets
- Predominantly greys and whites
- Coastal, art deco and French overtones
- Personal touches, such as lots of photos
- Furniture with cross legs, square or round, and classic detailing

Style

Retro style

Inspired by designers of fine furniture in the 50s, 60s and 70s, the retro look is all about textures, colour and timbers. Using timbers in different ways cuts costs, while still getting the look of solid timber. This style was the beginning of open planning in the home.

Elements of Retro style:
- Open spaces
- Textures
- Bold colour choices – browns, blues, oranges, purples, yellows, greens and reds
- Eclectic
- Focus on elegant simplicity with functionality
- Designer furniture pieces
- Classic modern pieces from the 50s, 60s or 70s
- Furniture typically has curved or circular forms
- Leather, shag rugs and bold patterns

Industrial style

Taking inspiration from the industrial era of history, this style is raw, exposed, edgy and rustic.

Think converted lofts, warehouses and studios with clean lines and hard finishes.

Elements of Industrial style:
- Different shades of black, white, grey and brown
- Exposed materials such as bricks, concrete, steel, metals and distressed timbers
- Rustic yet clean lines
- Vintage touches
- High ceilings
- Graphic artwork of vintage signs
- Industrial lighting

Boho style

There is more than one way to apply the Boho style. Pick your preference, as some of these elements can be used in varying degrees.

Elements of Boho style:
- Vintage leathers
- Macramé and crochet
- Natural textures
- Tribal influences
- Pillows and cushions
- Nature
- Rustic timbers
- Soft colours – whites, pinks, blues and greens, with natural linen colours
- Artwork is soft or can be done with a wild-west feel using cacti

Style

Coastal style

This style is laid-back, with a relaxed and calm feel. Think about holidays – colours of the sea, sand and light.

Elements of Coastal style:
- Soft colours – whites, greys, blues, greens and pinks
- Natural textures and fabrics
- Coastal elements such as coral and shells
- Timbers are rustic or bleached
- Matt finishes
- Limited metal touches
- Lighting elements are cane or simple lighting
- White rattan
- Natural stones such as limestone or sandstone
- Blacks as an accent

Chapter 4

Getting started

Getting started

So now that you have found your style, where do you start?

Begin by looking at what you already have and what you will need. Keeping transitional styles in mind, what can you repurpose or upcycle? Make a list of all the things you would like for your new style, even if you don't think you will need them. Once you have your list, you can start shopping!

You can start looking at second-hand pieces online. Not all items will appear when you want them, so it is important to be patient. There is always someone out there changing their look and getting rid of what they don't need, so you can be sure to find what you are looking for. Make sure you search across multiple websites, such as Gumtree, Facebook Marketplace and eBay, to give you the best opportunity to find what you're after.

Tip 1
Make a list of the items you will need to complete the look, then once you have your style you can start shopping!

Getting started

Check out kerbside items or any skip bins that you find. If you do see something you like in a skip, always ask first before you take the item.

Have a look at charity shops and other retailers for bargains – they might have just the right item on sale! Be prepared to think outside the box. And if there is something you just can't live without, be patient. I have never had to wait more than a month for a particular item to appear at the price I was willing to pay, so just keep at it and be ready to pounce when you see it.

Buying second-hand is not for the faint-hearted. You have to make quick decisions as it's pretty competitive out there. But if you stick to your list and use a bit of imagination, you will be ready when you need to be.

Tip 2
Keep your eyes peeled.

If you miss out on a piece, consider letting the seller know that if no one shows, you are still willing to pick it up. This once happened to me – I spotted a really old sofa that was a 50s art deco revival piece, solidly built but needing reupholstering. The buyer measured it but it would not fit in their home, so the seller contacted me and I picked it up with some help from a friend.

33

Chapter 5

Finding your pieces

Finding your pieces

In this chapter we'll look at how to find the right second-hand pieces in each category, from the big stuff down to the last lampshade.

Furniture

When you're searching for furniture online, the first thing to do is set up notifications or alerts for the pieces you want. This way, you will have the best chance of getting in first when an item is posted for sale.

Make sure you inspect photos of the furniture closely and ask the seller if there is any damage. Always be aware of what you are able to fix and what is beyond your ability. If you haven't done much restoration before, start with something that only requires a bit of filler and a paint job. This way, your confidence will grow as you finish your projects and you will feel brave enough to tackle something that is bigger or requires a little more attention.

Small things, like a loose leg, might just need some tightening of a screw or an extra washer on the screw because the wood has shrunk with age.

You can completely change the look of an item, especially if it is a vintage piece, by upcycling it. I once found a low-height 50s dresser that I added castors to and painted to turn it into an entertainment unit. Try to go for solid timber pieces if you can; they will always last much longer than other pieces.

Finding your pieces

Handles

If you don't like the handles on your furniture, consider changing them but be aware that handles are not cheap. They can easily add $50 to your purchase, unless you get them second-hand also.

The size of the holes for vintage handles are generally smaller than for modern ones, so finding replacements can be hard. If you want to change your handles, try spraying them in the paint colour of your choice. This is a much cheaper option. For timber handles, you can paint them at the same time as painting the rest of your piece.

If you want to change the position of the handles, you can fill the original holes with filler and redrill new holes. Scratches and chips are easily fixed with filler and paint, so you don't need to worry too much about any minor damage unless there is timber missing from the piece. Give these items a miss, unless you are up for the challenge of making major structural fixes.

Always keep any handles that you replace. You never know when you might be able to use them for another project or to replace a broken one.

Finding your pieces

Beds

Second-hand bedframes are perfectly fine; however, mattresses or ensembles require careful selection. Make sure that they are not stained and have had mattress protectors on them. Sometimes, second-hand beds have only been used for a guest room or for a short period of time.

I do suggest, as an added insurance, that if you do buy a second-hand mattress you vacuum and disinfect it with a suitable spray for upholstery, such as Glen 20. This will help to ensure it's as clean as it can be before you sleep on it.

Sofas and couches

For sofas and couches (or any large item), you must consider how you are going to get it home. You must be choosy and ask yourself a couple of questions before you purchase. Are the springs broken? Is it in good condition and without stains? Can it be easily reupholstered? Getting a sofa cleaned will cost around $100–200, so keep this in mind.

Tip 3
Buy solid built or vintage pieces.

Sofas that have been used in a formal living setting are the best to buy, as they about a third of the price of a new one; however, you will also pay the most for them. Cheap sofas are usually sold at such a low cost because they need extensive repairs or they are big bulky items that are hard to pick up and carry. Other large and heavy items, such as dining tables and bookcases, are often cheaper for the same reasons. Check whether the item can be taken apart for easy transport, and if not, ask the seller if they can deliver the item.

Finding your pieces

Another important consideration – and this might sound like a no-brainer – is to make sure that the item fits your space. You need to know the dimensions of your space before you buy. It's also a good idea to take your measuring tape with you when you go to look at the piece. If you live in an apartment, check that the item will fit in the lift or stairwell. I once had to get a sofa into a building with no lift and a stairwell that was old and too narrow to fit the sofa – in the end, it had to be squeezed through the second-floor window!

Tip 4
Know how big your area is and what size sofa will fit.

If you are going to reupholster a sofa, make sure you get it cheap. Depending on the style, a professional upholsterer is going to cost you, and this expense needs to be looked at as an investment. You need to love it for a long time!

Tip 5
Think outside the box; be creative.

Later in this book, there is a photo of a sofa I had professionally upholstered with a modern twist of colours. Because of the amount of timber in the piece, it was very heavy. My upholsterer was able to lighten the load by adjusting the timber frame and using polyester wadding instead of the existing wool batting. It took three of us to move the thing! It is such a classic, and I won't be selling it too soon in the future, that's for sure.

Accent chairs don't cost as much to reupholster as a sofa (we will talk more about upholstery in Chapter 7). Accent chairs are usually single chairs that make a statement. They can really make your interiors pop, so keep an eye out for them. Putting one in a guest bedroom will elevate the design to the next level.

Finding your pieces

Linen and blinds

Buy unused linen when you can. White linen works well with all styles, and you can add colour with your cushions and bed throws.

Tip 6
Buy unused linen when you can.

Sheets don't have to be white but neutral colours work best. If you want to have a colour, choose one of the accent colours you have in the room. An accent colour is a small amount of colour that enhances the overall colour scheme but does not overpower it.

When buying curtains, remember to measure the width and height of your window to make sure they fit. There are usually two lengths for curtains: 2,000 millimetres or 2,300 millimetres. Don't be put off by the longer length, as you can always re-hem to shorten them or raise your curtain rail.

Linen and blinds

Finding your pieces

It is best to buy blinds new, unless you only want a temporary fix. Blinds are fixed to the window in two ways: face fix or top fix. Face-fixed blinds are fitted to the wall or the side architraves, while top fixing means fitting the bracket to the underside of the architraves or onto the ceiling. You need to know which method is best for you so you get the right measurements. For example, if you want to limit the amount of light in the room, you might opt for face-fixing blinds so that the blind extends past the edges of the window to darken the room more effectively.

Venetian blinds can be shortened by removing some of the bottom slats. There are lots of videos available online if you are unsure how to do this or if you need help with measuring or fixing brackets.

Accessories and artwork

Accessories and artwork are usually the cheapest and easiest items to buy. There is often a lot to choose from, and again, you will need to know the measurements of your space to make sure the item fits.

A common error is that people choose artwork that is far too small for their walls. Ideally, the artwork should cover approximately two thirds of the width of the wall. This measurement can be broken up to include a number of smaller pieces along the wall, rather than one big piece. If the artwork is small, it might be better to group several pieces together to achieve a better balance between the artworks and the blank spaces around them.

You can also buy any canvas that is the right size for your space, even if you don't like the artwork on it. Try covering the canvas to suit your colour scheme using fabric and a staple gun.

If the frame of your artwork is not the right colour, consider taking the artwork out and spray-painting the frame. If it has been professionally framed or you don't want to disturb the print, tape up the frame, cover the glass and spray away.

Tip 7
Don't worry too much about frame colour.

Finding your pieces

Another option is to retain some of the original colour and only paint a portion of the frame using a paintbrush. For instance, if the frame is gold and has some nice detailing that you want to preserve, you could paint the outer edge in black to tie in with your colour scheme. Always look at the piece in terms of what is simpler and how you can use what you already have.

When removing the frame from an artwork, you might find that the glass is very thin and delicate. Make sure you have a solid, flat surface to place the glass on. Be careful not to put too much pressure on the glass. If it does break, you can get a replacement from a framer but it is not cheap. Lesson learned!

Accessories are usually easy to find second-hand, but always consider Kmart and other suitable retailers as well. I check out the major second-hand retailers online and see if they have what I'm looking for. If you do see something online that is new, copy the name of the item and try searching for it on the second-hand site – you might be able to find an identical item for a fraction of the price!

Finding your pieces

Hanging your artwork or mirrors

It is important to get the right hook for the job, so if you have plasterboard walls, use the appropriate hook for the weight of the item. It is important to know how much your piece weighs before you buy a hook. You can weigh your piece on domestic scales if you have them. I also make sure that I buy a hook that is designed to support more weight than I need, so I know it is going to stay up.

Tip 8
Make sure you know what size will fit your wall area or group frames together.

Finding your pieces

Rugs

There are usually two types of rugs available: wool and polyester/polypropylene.

Wool	Polyseter/polypropylene
• Lasts a long time. • Usually requires professional cleaning. • Costs more.	• Lasts a shorter amount of time. • Can be steam cleaned yourself. • Costs less.

Tip 9
Check out brand new rugs on sale.

People usually get rid of a rug because they either want a new look or have moved house and no longer need it.

You can pick up second-hand rugs for around $50 to $100. They are usually cleaned before selling, but look for any stains before you buy. If you can't find the rug you are looking for, you can always buy a brand-new one on sale. The rugs on sale can be quite a bargain!

Finding your pieces

The size of your rug is important. As a general rule, 1,600mm x 2,400mm suits a sitting area with a three-seater lounge and an accent chair. If you have a large sitting area that is bigger than three by three metres, you may need a rug that is 2,000mm x 3,000mm.

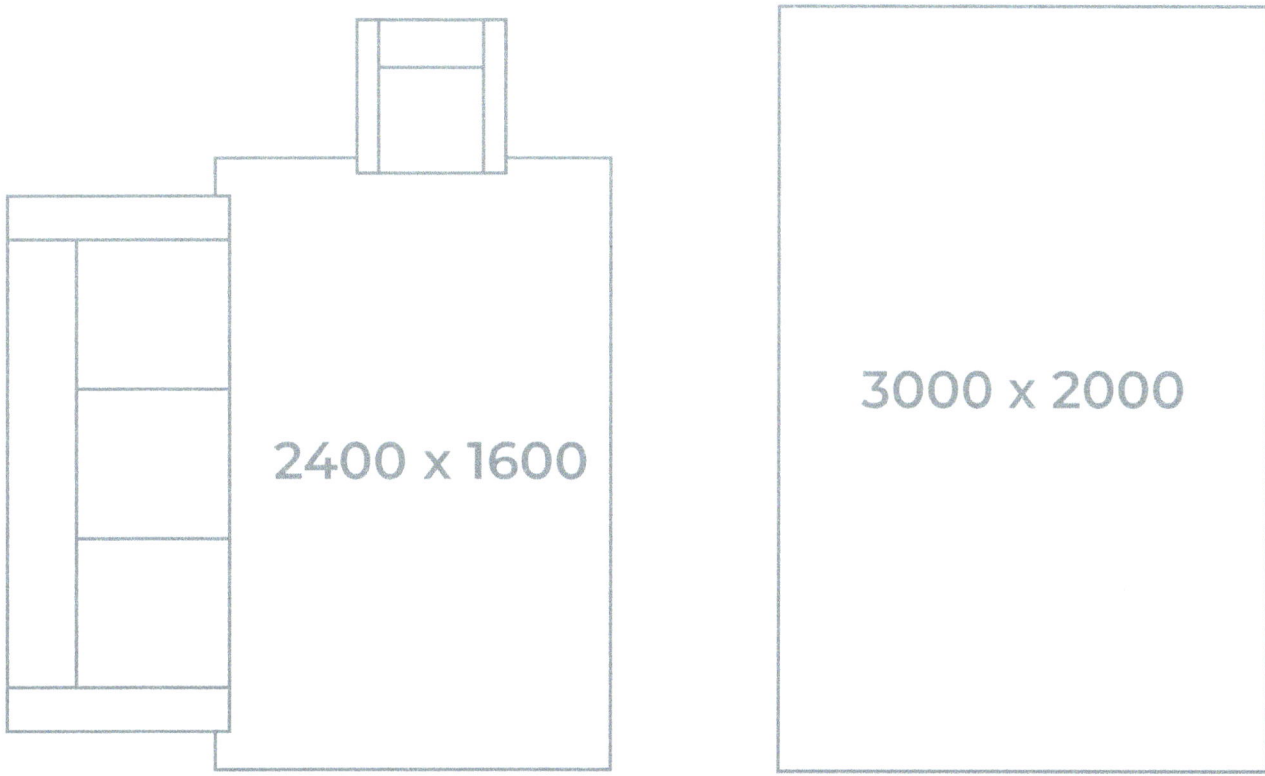

Map out the area you want to cover and measure the floor space so you have an idea of the size you need.

Rugs are a bit like artwork – most people tend to buy a rug that is too small for the space. I would generally not buy anything smaller than 1,600mm x 2,400mm, unless the rug was for a doorway (but not for the entryway – the rug in the entryway should be large enough to make a statement).

Finding your pieces

Lamps

Keep an open mind when looking for lamps. Lampshades are easy to change or buy second-hand in the colour you want. Shades do not last as long as the lamps, so it is not as important when buying; you can always get a new one in the style or colour you want for a cheap price.

I once had a single bedside lamp and was fortunate enough to find another that was the same, but with a black shade instead of a white one. I picked up two new shades for $2 each at a clearance sale. Problem solved!

Tip 10
Don't worry too much about the shade colour.

Tip 11
Buy lamps that are around 50cm to 60cm height they fit best for all areas.

Kitchenware

Finding your pieces

You can buy everything you need for the kitchen second-hand. Dinnerware that has hardly been used is a great buy. You can usually find everything from electrical goods that someone bought on a whim to cutlery that has never been used – even wedding gifts that were not quite what the bride wanted! Their loss is your gain.

Tip 12
Are there any chips or missing pieces to the set, and can you live with that?

Finding your pieces

Large electrical items

Fridges and freezers are hard to transport, so they are often fairly cheap to buy. Always ask if the seller can deliver. If not, as with large furniture, you will have to find a way to get it home – without throwing your back out! Washing machines are heavy but will fit in some cars. Make sure the item is secure, as accelerating or braking too hard can send the item through your back window or into the back of you, so be careful!

Tip 13
Look at reviews for any electrical item you are buying and know what to ask the seller, like, age, any problems?

Pickup or delivery

Before you agree to pick up an item, you need to know the dimensions of the object and the dimensions of your car. Know what you are able to carry and what must be delivered or picked up by other means.

Tip 14
Make sure you know what will fit in your car.

Sellers will sometimes offer to deliver for a small charge, or you can look for delivery drivers that provide this service using a ute or small truck. You can find these services in online directories or on second-hand pages. I usually avoid them though, as it can become pricey unless you have a couple of items in the area and you can arrange to have them picked up on the same day.

Tip 15
Always carry a tape measure when viewing items.

If you have a friend or relative with a ute, ask if you can borrow it and pay them some petrol money. Another option is to rent a ute for the day and use it to pick up everything you can.

Finding your pieces

Postal or courier delivery is also an option when buying online, although this means you don't get the chance to look at the piece in person first, so be careful about what you buy. You will also need to pay for the item before you have it picked up; discuss this with the seller in case this option doesn't suit them.

It is also wise to ask the seller before pickup if there are any stairs you will need to negotiate, especially if the piece is heavy or large.

Using your imagination

You need to be adaptable when looking at second-hand furniture or finding a piece on the kerbside. For example, I once found a coffee table with no top and only the frame. I turned it into an ottoman by painting the base and upholstering the frame (there is a finished photo of this item later in the book). It looks fantastic! So, think outside the box and use your imagination.

Tip 16
Just because it is a bedside doesn't mean it always has to be a bedside.

Tip 17
Use your imagination and be creative.

Finding your pieces

Realising you bought the wrong item

If you have bought something that you feel was a mistake and you just can't make it work, you have a couple of options:
- Resell the piece as is
- If you want to make a little more money, upcycle it by painting or staining it and then reselling it.

The vast majority of people are time-poor or just don't want to deal with repainting, so think about what buyers want. Remember to check out the prices that similar items are selling for on the second-hand market and crunch the numbers.

Tip 18
Resell anything that just doesn't work or if you have bitten off more than you can chew to fix a piece.

Chapter 6

Painting

Painting

Paint, paint and more paint!

It's amazing how much you can transform your piece with a little paint!

I am by no means a professional painter and I don't tout myself as one, but I have painted with chalk paint and water-based enamels and I can achieve a pretty high-quality finish. It takes a little bit of practice, but by the time you finish your first piece, you will be hooked.

Chalk paint is soft, so you will need to seal it with wax or a clear matt finish. If you need the piece to be hard-wearing, such as a dining table or the top of a dresser, the clear finish will make it a lot more durable.

There are many different types of paint these days, so you are only limited by your imagination. There are gold paints, copper finishes, stone, suede or metallic, just to name a few.

Painting

Things you will need for painting:
- Sugar soap wipes
- Rags
- Painters' tape
- Drop sheet
- Sandpaper – 120 grit, 150 grit and 180 grit
- Paintbrushes – 25mm and 50mm
- Small roller kit suitable for enamel paints
- Screwdrivers – Philips head and flat, for taking off handles
- Paint tin opener
- Hammer for putting the paint tin lid back on
- Plastic bag for keeping your brushes and roller wet between coats
- Stirrer for the paint.

Painting

Some rules on preparing furniture for painting

Here I will share with you some of my rules for preparing pieces for painting which have worked for me. Give it go!

1. Look at the piece and decide which parts will be painted and which will not.

   It might not always be clear where the paint should start and end. For example, I completed a bedside table that had a pull-out tray and a drawer underneath. The tray was in good condition, but it jutted out more and I would have had to paint either the whole tray or just the edge, which was tricky as the paint might have bled onto the surface that I didn't want painted. I made the decision not to paint the tray as I could remove it while painting the rest of the piece.

2. Remove the handles and anything else that you don't want painted.

3. Clean your piece with sugar soap, fill any chips and sand it back.

   I use Selleys Sugar Soap Wipes to clean the piece. I then fill any chips with Selleys Rapid Filler, which dries quickly and is paintable. After waiting for the required time you can then sand your piece to give it a smooth finish. I use 120 or 150 grit sandpaper, depending on the condition and whether there are any grooves or marks that need to be sanded out. The higher the number on the sandpaper, the finer the sandpaper will be.

4. Clean the piece one more time.

   Once you have sanded and you are happy with the finish, clean the piece again to make sure all dust is removed from the item. Check that it is thoroughly dry before you paint.

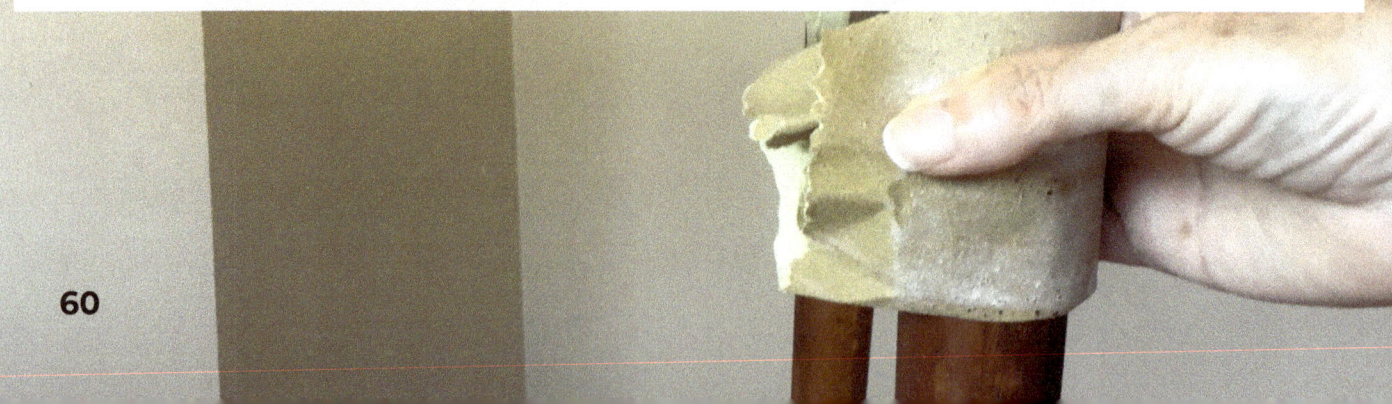

Brushes and rollers

It's a good idea to buy medium-priced brushes, as cheaper ones will lose their bristles and ruin your paint finish. Rollers come in different 'naps' (the length of the fibres on the roller), so you need to choose the one that suits your paint. Roller manufacturers will specify whether the roller is suitable for walls and ceiling paint – this is usually for low-sheen paints. For enamels, you will need a roller that is suitable for gloss and semi-gloss and has a shorter nap.

Painting

Primer

The number-one rule for painting is to always use a primer, as it will seal the existing finish and help the new finish to stick to the piece. Remember, prep is everything! It is just not worth it to go without a primer, especially when you have gone to all the trouble of painting the piece and find you have to start all over again!

Start with an undercoat primer. Chalk paint manufacturers say you don't need to sand or prime with chalk paint but trust me, it saves money in the long run. Chalk paint will cover the piece but if you are painting a light colour over a dark one, you will need three to four coats and chalk paint is expensive, so an undercoat primer is worth its weight in gold.

Water-based primers are best, unless you have a particularly dark piece that has been stained, then you will need a primer that has a stain blocker in it. The 4-in-1 range from British Paints is a good choice, as is the one-step water-based range from Dulux. Both products are thick and easy to use and have great coverage. I have used some cheaper brands before but have not been happy with them. You might give them a try and decide for yourself.

As a general rule, you can't apply water-based paints on top of oil-based paints, so you will need to prime these items as well. Let's face it, it's often hard to know what type of paint has been used on an item bought second-hand. If the item has been previously painted and the paint is chipping off in small pieces, then this is a sign that the paint is oil-based. On the other hand, if the paint chip is stretchy, it is most likely water-based. You can also try the methylated spirits test: rub the item with methylated spirits on a cloth to see if the paint transfers or becomes sticky. If this happens, then the paint is water-based.

Gloss levels and colour for water-based enamels

Chalk paint has a matt finish and is all the rage at the moment. If you are using water-based enamels, they will generally come in semi-gloss or gloss. Dulux now has a low-sheen level which is perfect for a matt look. The lower the sheen level, the more forgiving it is on the appearance of any imperfections in the paintwork or the piece itself. Low-sheen is only available for light colours or those marked with a W on the colour chips.

When you look at the colour wall, each colour will have a name and a letter or symbol beside it. These letters tell you which base the colour is available in.

White base

Extra bright base

Deep base

Ultra deep base

Brighter colours require deeper or brighter bases. This means that the paint base already has some tint in it, so when your colour is mixed there is enough room to put the tint into the can.

You don't need to worry too much about which base you need. The kind people who tint the paint will help you out and make sure you get the right base for the right colour. All you need to do is pick the colour.

Tip 19
All bases that are not white are more expensive to compensate for the extra tint inside the can.

Painting

If you want a Hamptons look, there are a couple of colours in the Dulux range that go well. Hamptons white is a creamier white than you might think. Try Dulux Natural White, which is a little creamier than a stark white like Dulux Vivid White, or if you want a grey-white, try Dulux White on White. Vivid White has no tint in it, and it is as pure a white as they come. It's good for a Scandinavian look but can also be used for a Hamptons style if you want bright white furniture.

If you have tiled white floors, go for Natural White furniture as it will give you a warmer feel than Vivid White. If you have timber floors, you can use either a warm white or a cool white. The difference between the two won't matter, as the timber will give you enough warmth in the room.

Example of a cool colour scheme

Example of a warm colour scheme

If you have timber flooring with yellow tones and you choose a cool white, you may find that it will bring out the blue undertone in the white. This depends on the light in the room, but is not so important for a piece of furniture, as you can usually live with whichever you choose.

Tip 20
The more you paint, the better you will become!

A small piece that is slightly off-colour in a room full of furniture will not be noticeable as the eye tends to blend things. You might only notice if the piece is right next to another piece that has a different tone.

If you have bought two pieces of furniture from different suppliers, they will probably be in different whites. My advice is to not worry about it too much, but do try to stick to either warm or cool palettes where possible. Warm whites generally have a mixture of red and yellow in their undertone, while cool whites have blue or green undertones.

The easiest way to see which undertone your white has is to put the swatch up against a pure white. The undertone will be more obvious, and if you are not sure, place both side-by-side against the pure white.

Painting

The painting process

Now that you have the primer on and you have let it dry for the required time, you are ready to paint your first topcoat.

Enamel paint

Water-based enamels will dry fast, especially if it is hot and humid, so pick a cooler and drier time of day. Generally, this will be first thing in the morning or mid-afternoon. You can add a hot-weather thinner to the enamel if you want to speed up the drying time.

When you use enamel paint, it is important to keep a wet edge and not go back over anything that is starting to dry – otherwise, you will end up with an uneven gloss finish. If this does happen, use a wet cloth to smooth it out as the water in the cloth will soften the paint again. Wait for it to dry and touch up that area with another coat.

Once you have painted the area, lay the area off. This means to finish off with an unloaded roller or brush, just lightly touching the surface while only brushing in one direction. This is particularly important for big flat areas. For smaller areas, it is not so important to lay the area off. With water-based enamels it is best to load the brush or roller to cover the areas quickly and smoothly.

Allow enough time according to the paint can instructions before adding the second coat. Some people ask why a second coat is needed. The simple answer is that you don't always cover the piece evenly when doing the first coat, so the second is to even it out. Plus, a second coat will add durability to the finish.

I usually like to brush on the first coat and use only the roller on the second coat. Once dry, you will need to check the piece for any areas that need touching up with a third coat, especially if you are doing a white colour. This final touch fixes any imperfections in your painting and evens out any brushstrokes.

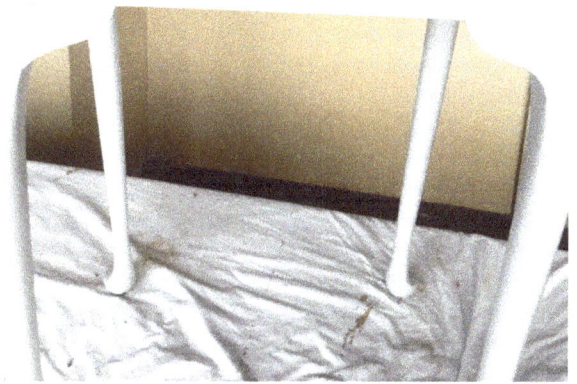

Put any hardware back on the piece once it has fully dried. Enamel paints take approximately seven days to harden, so for best results put the hardware back after this time. Refrain from putting any items on the piece while it is still hardening as they might stick to the paint. Once seven days have passed you can then use your piece.

I sometimes get asked, 'Does water-based paint wash off in the rain?' The answer is no – once it has dried it can only be removed with a solvent.

Painting

Chalk paint

Chalk paint is thick and dries quickly, so you will need to work fairly fast. If you go back over it too soon you will get a rough finish. Once the coat has dried, use clear wax to seal the finish by using a round brush and a swirling motion to apply. Wax small areas at a time, wait a couple of minutes and then buff off. Wax will harden in time for a durable finish.

Chalk paint is cheaper if you make your own. There are different recipes on the internet but the one below is what I like to use. It can be hard to find calcium carbonate, but it is available from home brewery shops.

Chalk paint recipe

- 2 parts acrylic paint
- 1 part calcium carbonate

Mix paint and calcium carbonate together until the mixture has a smooth consistency.

This paint will dry in 30 minutes. Store chalk paint in a glass or plastic container with a tight-fitting lid.

It is important to check whether your furniture piece has been waxed. If it has, the paint might not dry on it or adhere to it. How do you tell? When you wash it, you will notice that the surface goes milky. This is a sure sign the piece has been waxed. You could also try the fingernail trick – when you scratch it with your fingernail, see if it makes a mark.

To get the wax off, use a good amount of methylated spirits applied with fine steel wool to help loosen the wax, then wipe down your piece with a cloth. You may have to do this a few times to get all the wax off. Once the wax is no longer transferring any colour onto the cloth, you will know you have got it all off.

Painting

Whitewashing

I have mentioned whitewashing in the previous chapters, so let's have a look at it in more detail. Whitewashing gives an interesting and enhanced finish and works a treat on timber that is too dark for your style. Paint is added to the wood to either lighten it or add colour, like a stain. Whitewashing allows the wood grain to show through, as it is a transparent finish. It is easy to apply but requires a little bit of patience, as it is a longer process than painting.

You will need water-based paint – it doesn't matter whether it is aqua enamel or just water-based wall paint. The recipe is 50/50 water and paint. You need to apply it with a brush or cloth (I prefer a cloth) and work in small sections, as the paint will dry very fast. Apply the paint then rub it off with a clean cloth.

It's best to apply one thin coat than too thick a coat. Wait for your finish to dry and decide then whether you want to do another coat. If you are unhappy with the colour, you can always add more coats but you can't take it off once it's dry (unless you sand the piece and start again). So, start with one coat and work from there. Remember, the more coats you add, the harder it will be to see the wood grain.

Once you are happy with the finish, you will need to seal it with wax or a clear matt topcoat for durability. Dulux have one that works well and I use this on tabletops or anything that will be used regularly. Wax will work on items that you don't use all the time, like a buffet or bedside. Just remember that wax will mark if you put really hot items on it.

Wax comes in different colours and can be applied to areas of the furniture you want to enhance or seal. Clear wax is used if you just want to seal the item and not add any colour, and dark wax can be applied to the detailing of a piece to create an antique feel. Gilding wax comes in metallic colours – gold, silver and bronze – and can be applied to enhance details. I found one called Rub 'n Buff that works a treat! A word of caution, though – you will need to remove the wax from your piece later if you wish to repaint it.

Distressing your piece

If you want a more rustic look, you can distress your piece by rubbing back some of the finish with 120 grit sandpaper. Remember, the lower the grit number the coarser the sandpaper. You only want to take off some of the paint, so start by taking off only a little and build up. You can do this if you have used chalk paint or aqua enamels but haven't yet waxed or added any clear coats. Chalk paint is soft, so distressing can be done pretty easily; aqua enamels harden in seven days, so do the distressing in the first couple of days after painting.

Painting

Putting it into practice

Let me take you through a piece I did. I started with a set of timber drawers.

Look for any imperfections so you will know if you need to fill anything. Take off any hardware like handles. Wash down the piece with sugar soap, let dry, fill any imperfections, then sand and clean any dust off.

Then it was onto priming the piece for painting.

And finally, the last coat of paint.

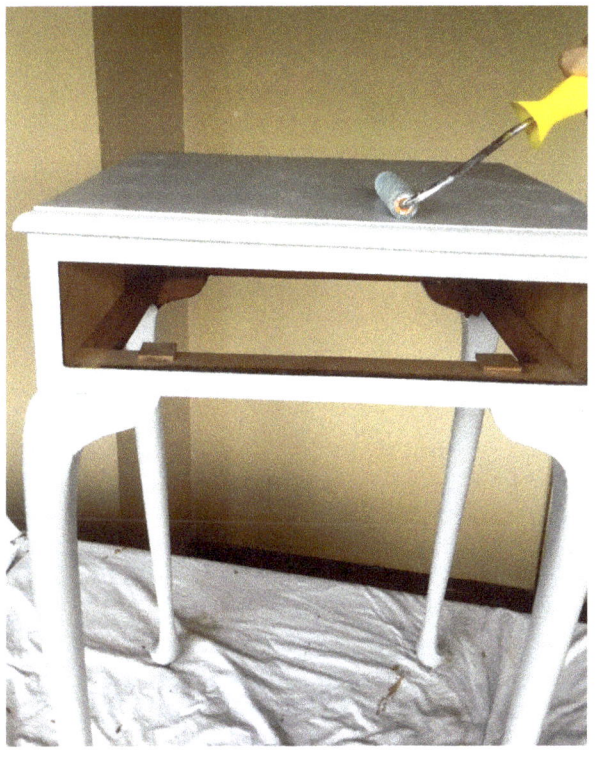 

Chapter 7

Upholstery

Upholstery

Getting started in upholstery

Upholstery is one of those things that people think they can't do, but it's really not that difficult. All you need to do is stick to the KISS method: keep it simple, stupid! To keep it simple, look for furniture that will minimise the amount of work required – for example, the back upholstery and seat upholstery are not connected, so there is no stitching involved.

Again, I am no expert when it comes to upholstery. When I was learning how to recycle furniture, I did a lot of research on DIY upholstery and watched a lot of videos about pieces similar to the one I was going to work on, such as a chair or an ottoman. Most of the items you will need for upholstery are available here in Australia, and there are DIY upholstery supplies available to order online.

When buying pieces to upholster, you can follow the way it has been covered or make some changes. For example, perhaps the item didn't have an upholstered back, but there is enough timber to upholster a panel on the back to give it a new look.

Always preserve any old upholstery and keep it for the pattern, and take out all the staples or tacks. Clean the piece and follow the painting rules if you are going to paint the frame. Finish the frame completely, especially if you are using chalk paint with wax or a clear coat, then move onto upholstering it.

> **Tip 21**
> Before buying furniture to reupholster, take a look at how you will do the upholstering.

Upholstery

Things you will need:

- Staple gun (electric or manual)
- Plenty of staples that fit with your gun
- Staple remover
- Small hammer
- Web stretcher
- Glue gun with trigger and glue sticks
- Foam
- Webbing for seating
- Wadding
- Calico for holding the webbing down
- Spray adhesive
- Gimp to cover the staples (unless they are on the underside of the piece).

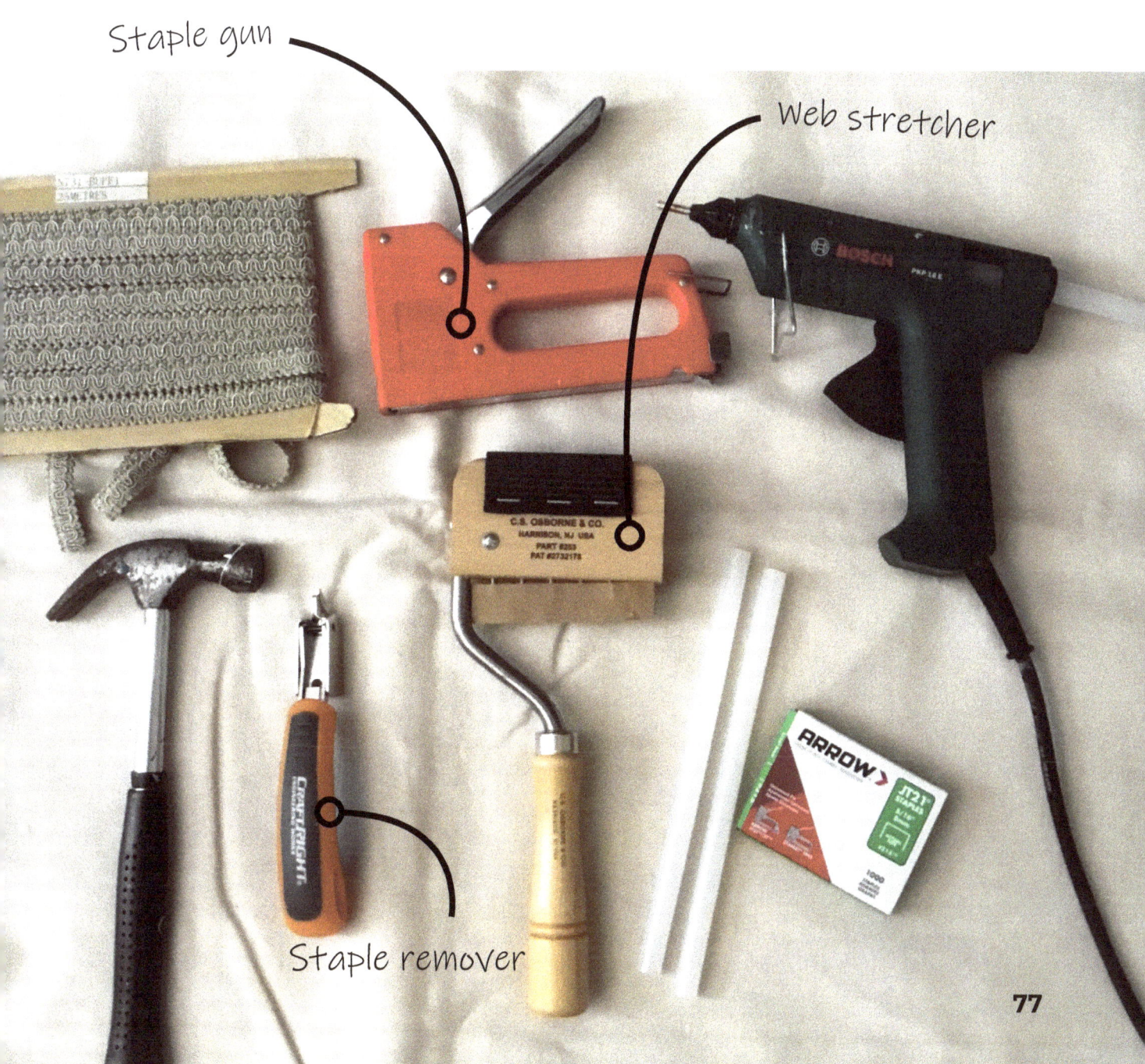

Upholstery

Fabric

Choosing fabric can be a bit tricky if you are not familiar with your style. Look at lots of images for inspiration and try to keep to a neutral palette, as this will give you the greatest longevity.

If you want an accent piece then you can be bold, but go for something you love so you can incorporate it into any new style if your style changes. With an accent piece, choose a fabric that is the epitome of that style (it can be a modern version of that style). For example, if you want a Hamptons look, go for a stripe, nautical, or classic fleur-de-lis pattern.

Tip 22
Try draping the fabric loosely over the piece to get an idea.

Upholstery

Fabrics for upholstery are not the same as fabrics for soft furnishings like curtains and cushions. Upholstery fabric is hard-wearing for pieces you use all the time. For an accent piece that is mainly used as decoration with occasional use, the fabric doesn't have to be as hard-wearing.

Avoid stripes when you are just starting out. You have to make sure you have the stripe lined up perfectly, and this can be really tricky! The same goes for many patterns – when choosing fabric for a chair, always imagine how it will sit on the seat of the chair and which features of the pattern should be in the middle of the chair.

When cutting your fabric, make sure you have the pattern running the same way. Before you cut, double-check to see that everything is right. If you do make a mistake, keep the fabric for another smaller job later. And don't worry; it's all part of the learning experience!

Chapter 8

Budget

Budget

The budget I used is a rough guide for what you can achieve and the prices you can expect to pay second-hand. For the experiment, I found I could fit out a three-bedroom home with furniture and some homewares for under $2,000. Pretty impressive, I think!

These are the items I based my budget on (no whitegoods):

- ☐ 3 beds
- ☐ 6 bedsides
- ☐ 6 lamps
- ☐ 2 rugs
- ☐ Linen and towels
- ☐ Kitchenware for 4
- ☐ Hall table or entry table
- ☐ Home office desk and chair
- ☐ Three-seater lounge
- ☐ Accent chair
- ☐ 5 pieces of artwork
- ☐ 2 bar stools
- ☐ Entertainment unit
- ☐ Cushions and accessories
- ☐ All other items suitable for Hamptons style

Budget

The prices below are a general guide to what you can expect to get for your money when buying second-hand, depending on style. Keep in mind that anything that doesn't need paint or is a particularly good example of a style will probably cost more, as you are paying for convenience and quality.

Item	Cost
Beds - Queen	$150
- Double	$70
- Single	$70
Bedsides x 2	$100–$200
Lamps x 2	$20–$120
Rugs - Wool	$100–$200
- Polyester	$40–$80
Hall table	$100–$120
TV units	$60–$100
Home office desk	$60–$100
Office chair	$40–$100
Lounge	$100–$300
Formal lounge (little use)	$500
Accent chairs	$20–$100
Buffets	$50–$200
Coffee table	$50
Lamp table	$25–$50
Artwork	$5–$25
Artwork large	$50–$100
Bar stools	$10–$20
Dining tables	$30–$100
Dining chair x 6	$60–$100
Dining table and chairs (set)	$80–$200
Linen queen size	$100
Towels Sheridan set	$100
Kitchenware	$10–$100
Small fridge/freezer	$125–$250

Budget

Bargain buys

Let me show you some of the items I've found on a second-hand budget.

Bedsides $35 each, lamps $30 for the pair, shades on clearance $2 each, bed $70, artwork (from a charity shop) $10.

Drop table kerbside pickup and painted, artwork $50 a pair from a second-hand website.

Budget

Dining table bought for $300, second-hand chairs bought online that I had reupholstered after I painted the frames.

Desk picked up for free, painted and new handles added. Chair bought second-hand in a set of 6 for $50, painted and reupholstered. All from a second-hand website.

Budget

Sofa bought on sale for $500, coffee table $30 and painted myself. Matching side table bought separately for $15 and painted myself. Side chair, leather with stainless steel base, bought for $50. All bought from a second-hand website. Rug bought new, $139 on sale.

Two of three chairs purchased for $50, reupholstered and painted frames black. Artwork is fabric applied over an existing canvas I had, $50.

Budget

Chapter 9

Before and afters

Before and afters

I have learned so much from this second-hand experiment, and I hope you have taken some ideas and inspiration from this book.

Here are some before-and-after photos of items that I have bought and repurposed for this experiment. My last word is that if you don't like a piece you have finished, repaint it, upcycle it again or sell it! But whatever you do, have fun and give it a go!

Found on the kerbside, an office chair with a broken gas base. I took the base off and replaced the legs with Queen Anne-style ones and repainted the frame. I had the chair reupholstered in new fabric.

Before

Before and afters

Chair bought for $50 from a second-hand website, painted and reupholstered.

Before

Bought second-hand for $35, I repainted this table for a classic Hamptons-style look. This piece was a great find, as it has some detailing on the legs.

Before

Before and afters

Ottoman bought second-hand for $70, painted and reupholstered.

Before

Picked up for free from a second-hand website, painted and legs added.

Before

Before and afters

One of three chairs bought for $50, painted and reupholstered.

Before

Kerbside find for free, repainted for use as outdoor plant stands.

Before

Before and afters

Pair of bedsides picked up from a second-hand website for $50, painted white.

Before

Coffee table bought for $15 from a second-hand website, painted with white enamel and then with three other intermittent colours for a coastal look.

Before

Before and afters

Bought on second-hand website for $50 as the previous buyer couldn't pick it up as it was very wide and didn't fit through his doorway. This is the heavy Art Deco sofa transformed for Art Deco 1950s to 21st Century chic and a lot lighter. Professionally reupholstered and legs painted black.

Before

Found on the kerbside as a frame only, possibly a coffee table previously and converted to an ottoman coffee table and painted the legs white.